THE
I CHING
COMPANION

*An Answer for
Every Question*

JILL RICHARDS

SAMUEL WEISER, INC.
York Beach, Maine

First published in 1999 by
SAMUEL WEISER, INC.
Box 612
York Beach, ME 03910-0612
www.weiserbooks.com

Library of Congress Cataloging-in-Publication Data

Richards, Jill.
    The I Ching companion : an answer for every question
/ Jill Richards.
        p. cm.
    ISBN 1-57863-130-0 (pbk. : alk. paper)
        1. I ching.   I. Title.
PL2464. Z7R53 1999
299´.51282--dc21   99-30326
                                                              CIP

VG
Typeset in 11.5 point Truesdell
Cover art is a Chinese painting, *Two Puja Bodhisattvas Burning
Incense*, ca. 951–953. Nelson Atkins Museum of Art, Kansas City,
MO (gift of Mr. C. T. Loo).

Cover and text design by Kathryn Sky-Peck
The part title art, The I Ching Mandala by Walter Boye, used by
kind permission.

PRINTED IN THE UNITED STATES OF AMERICA

06 05 04 03 02 01 00 99
7 6 5 4 3 2 1

*The paper used in this publication meets the minimum requirements of the
American National Standard for Information Sciences—Permanence of
Paper for Printed Library Materials Z39.48-1992 (R1997).*

To Walter

Thank you very much
Thank you very much
Thank you very much

CONTENTS

PREFACE

The *I Ching* translation I refer to and quote from throughout this work is the Richard Wilhelm/Cary F. Baynes edition. Most translations of the *I Ching*, or *Book of Changes*, are translations of a book of oracles. Richard Wilhelm translated the *I Ching* in the form in which he recognized it—a book of Law.

The first section of this study guide gives a short description of the *I Ching*. The second section gives step-by-step instructions on how to consult the *I Ching*. The final section is similar in form to a concordance. Because of the ambiguity with which Americans view words such as "north," "south," "east," "west," "superior man," "cross the great water,"etc., I feel it is beneficial to understand what the *I Ching* means by these terms. Descriptions of frequently used terms and phrases are, therefore, quoted from the book. Page numbers are listed for easy reference. When referring to "man" and "mankind" as a species, I use the terms "human" and "humankind," to remain gender neutral. When quoting the *I Ching*, the original text references to "man" and "mankind" are unchanged.

The *I Ching* is one of the oldest continuously used documents in the history of humankind. I have prepared this guide with the hope that it may be of assistance to all who are attracted to the beauty and wisdom of the words found in this book of antiquity.

Namasté
JILL RICHARDS

INTRODUCTION

My study of the *I Ching* began in 1976 under the guidance of my friend and teacher, Walter Boye. Two years later, Walter began a most enlightening walk over the length and breadth of America, 5,200 miles. He carried the *I Ching* every step of the way as a symbol of its presence. (Walter met a yoga master under whom he wished to study. The walk was given to Walter, by the master, as a prerequisite to the class.) During that journey, one that took 15 $^1/_2$ months to complete, I drove the support vehicle and spent a great many hours studying the *I Ching*. Walter had an idea for an aide to understanding the *Book of Changes*, one that I pursued while traveling across the country. To the Western student of the *I Ching*, much of the terminology is unfamiliar. After reading and rereading the book four times (I spent much free time reading while Walter was walking), I composed a list of the most frequently used words and phrases, with accompanying descriptions quoted directly from the book. It became a tremendous aid to my own understanding of a most remarkable document. I would like to offer it to all who aspire to understand the *I Ching*.

"How do I consult the *I Ching*?" is a question frequently presented to me. At the back of the Wilhelm-Baynes edition, there are directions for consulting the book, but often the terminology can be confusing for those who are new to the work. I have thus prepared step-by-step instructions for beginners, to guide them through the consulting process. These contain valuable information for anyone interested in the *I Ching*.

Many very detailed books have been written about the *I Ching*. This book gives a brief description of its origin, how the work is set up, how it is used, and an interesting account of how Richard Wilhelm translated it from Chinese into German. Those wishing to explore the history and structure of the *I Ching* more deeply have a wealth of information accessible to them in libraries and bookstores. My intent here is to make the consulting process easier and more accessible to all, and to make the key words and phrases used repeatedly throughout the *I Ching* understandable.

The words and ideas presented here derive from my *I Ching* studies. The words work for me and I hope they work for you. More important, however, is their objective. The objective of life is the same for everyone: to attain a place wherein we are more content and at peace than any other—a place to which nothing can be added, and from which nothing need be taken away. That place is peace of mind. It is a psychological, not an external, condition. With peace of mind, there are no distracting thoughts. Distractions are questions, and questions are answers sought. Our work is to convert questions (negative energy) into knowing (positive energy). Bringing questions to resolution is the way to peace of mind. The *I Ching* can help us do just that.

> . . . *the superior man, whenever he has to make or do something, consults the Changes, and he does so in words. It takes up his communications like an echo; neither far nor near, neither dark nor deep exist for it, and thus he learns of the things of the future* (I Ching, p. 314).

My teacher, Walter Boye, was once asked what it was that he sought to leave with his audiences when lecturing on the *I Ching*. Walter replied: "The possibility of something else." The possibility of something else gives hope to humankind. The *I Ching* gives hope. May the following work leave you with the possibility of something other than what you may have considered before.

Acknowledgments

Many heartfelt thanks to:

Walter Boye, Josh Shirvanian, Jesse
Moore, Roger Bills, Jamie Richards, Hoyt
Jeffers, Mary Jane, Donald and Danielle,
Carolynne, and Sri Sathya Sai Baba

The Book of Changes contains a fourfold tao of the holy sages. In speaking, we should be guided by its judgments; in actions, we should be guided by its changes; in making objects, we should be guided by its images; in seeking an oracle, we should be guided by its pronouncements.

—I Ching, p. 314

1

What Is the I Ching?

MY FRIEND, WALTER, a student and teacher of the *I Ching*, was scheduled to present a lecture about the *Book of Changes*. Due to a typographical error in the local newspaper, the same evening, time, and location were incorrectly listed for another speaker as well. As people began arriving for the lecture, Walter discovered the mistake and explained the error to the assembling audience. He informed them that his topic was the *I Ching* and invited people to stay.

An hour into the lecture someone politely interrupted to ask, "What is this thing?"

"What thing?" Walter replied.

"This *I Ching* thing."

Realizing that the gentleman was unfamiliar with the *I Ching*, Walter reflected for a moment and then replied with a hearty laugh, "It's a good book!"

THE ORIGIN OF THE *I CHING*

I Ching (pronounced Yee Jing), or *Book of Changes* ("I" means change, "Ching" means book or classic) is one of the oldest Chinese works. The basic symbols used in the *I Ching* have been found recorded on bone oracles from early antiquity. King Wên, father of the founder of the Chou Dynasty (1150-249 B.C.), is commonly attributed with first committing the text of the *I Ching* to calligraphy. For over a thousand years, many historical personalities, including King Wên's son (the Duke of Chou) and Confucius, have been credited with contributing to its completed form.

A BOOK OF ORACLES, WISDOM, LAW

Most people familiar with the *I Ching* use it, or originally used it, as a book of oracles. When you direct a question to the *I Ching*, you invoke an answer. If you are assisted by the answer you receive, you will return to the book as other questions arise. Through repeated use, the book reveals its wisdom. By studying the *I Ching* as a book of wisdom, you ultimately come to see it as a book of Law. As my teacher Walter Boye said:

> *It is the Law we seek. Once we know the Law we must survive within, we are free to do that. Until then we waste energy.*

BOOKS I, II, AND III

The Wilhelm-Baynes translation of the *I Ching* consists of three parts, or books. Book I, The Text, is used when consulting the *I Ching*. Book II, The Material, explains the terminology and the structure of the work. Book III, The Commentaries, presents the text in Book I, along with further commentaries, or explanations, of the words and images.

When employing the *I Ching* as a book of oracles, you will use Book I almost exclusively. If, after reading the text, you do not understand particular words or images, Book III offers further explanations. As the material becomes familiar to you and you want to investigate further, you can read and study Book II.

RICHARD WILHELM'S TRANSLATION

Richard Wilhelm lived in China and studied Chinese for over twenty years. Over a period of several years, with the help of Lao Nai-hsüan, his honored teacher, he translated the *I Ching* from Chinese into his native German. His German words were then given to a Chinese student of German who was unfamiliar with the *I Ching*. He translated the text back into Chinese. That Chinese translation was then read by the masters in China, who either accepted or rejected the manuscript as a true representation of the original text. Wilhelm then corrected his German translation, until the masters confirmed that the work conveyed the same information contained in the *I Ching*. In that way, Wilhelm authenticated his choice of words. The masters were actually choosing the German

Figure 1. Richard Wilhelm. Courtesy Harmen Mesker.

words, although they only knew Chinese. When the Masters accepted the corrected translation as truly reflecting the original Chinese text, Wilhelm knew that his German translation was accurate.

While most translations of the *I Ching* represent the work as a book of oracles, Wilhelm dealt with it as a book of Law, making his translation the best translation to date.

2

How Do I Consult the I Ching?

THE COIN ORACLE

1 *Preparation:* When consulting the *I Ching*, you need not use ritual, although it can serve a purpose. (Hopefully, you do not "throw" the *I Ching*.) You may choose to sit in a quiet place and spread a cloth in front of you. You will need a copy of the book, three pennies, a pad of paper and a pen(cil). You may wish to light a candle and take a few minutes to clear your mind. Whatever your preparation, the amount of time spent in ritual helps to concentrate your mind and prepares you to be receptive to the words of the *I Ching*.

2 *Write down your question:* People frequently think they know what their question is and therefore see no need to write it down. However, when they finally articulate their thought, it may not be a question at all. For example, "It's about my family" is not a question. In order to make certain that you know what your question is, write it down. The answer is often revealed by the time your distraction is formed into a question.

The more specific your question, the more specific the answer will be. Be as specific as you can. If you do not have a specific question, however, the *I Ching* can still help. I often ask, "What information does the *I Ching* want to give to me at this time?"

Do not ask a question to which you already know the answer. Do not importune.

Ultimately, the question you are seeking is the question that, if answered, will leave you in a state without questions. Having no more questions, you will have achieved peace of mind. Peace of mind is your objective.

3 *Shake three pennies in cupped hands and let them fall:* Shaking the coins in cupped hands allows the coins to fall freely, without manipulation. Tao (pronounced *dow*) is allowed to enter into the process. While shaking the coins, it is most beneficial either to keep your mind at rest or to concentrate on your question. In that way, you are rendered most receptive to the answer.

The means by which the wisdom of the *I Ching* is imparted is equally available to all people. In the United States, copper pennies are used, as they are available to all Americans. Coins of small denomination were used by the Chinese people for the same reason. Chinese, or other, coins may be used, but they are not necessary.

4 *The value 2 is given to "heads" and the value 3 is given to "tails":* There is at least one good reason for this. We normally attribute a higher value to the head of a coin than we do to its reverse

side. Therefore, a lesser value is assigned to "heads" and a greater value is assigned to "tails." This allows us to consider something other than what we have considered before. It frees our minds and better prepares us to hear the words of the *I Ching*.

5 *The possible resulting numerical combinations are 6, 7, 8, 9:*

Heads = 2   Tails = 3

9	**─O─**	old yang
8	**── ──**	young yin
7	**────**	young yang
6	**─X─**	old yin

The "x" and "o" in the above chart indicate changing lines; they will change into their opposites. Make certain to mark the old yin (6) line and old yang (9) line with an "x" and an "o," respectively. This will be explained in greater detail a little further on.

6 *Add the values of the coins and draw either a broken or a solid line:* Use the example in number 5 to draw the lines. If, for example, the fall of the coins results in 3 heads (2 + 2 + 2 = 6), indicate that by drawing a changing (old yin) line (**─X─**). If the fall of the coins results in 2 heads and 1

tail (2 + 2 + 3 = 7), indicate that by drawing a young yang line (——). One head and 2 tails (2 + 3 + 3 = 8) are indicated by drawing a young yin line (– –). Three tails (3 + 3 + 3 = 9) are indicated by drawing a changing (old yang) line (–⊖–). Remember to indicate the changing lines with an "x" or an "o."

7 *Shake and drop the coins five more times:* This will allow you to construct a hexagram, a sign consisting of six lines. The first line is always the bottom line (base or foundation), and all following lines are built on top of each other. Example:

(2 + 2 + 3 = 7)	——	6th, or top, line
(2 + 2 + 2 = 6)	–✗–	5th line
(3 + 3 + 3 = 9)	–⊖–	4th line
(3 + 3 + 2 = 8)	– –	3rd line
(3 + 3 + 3 = 9)	–⊖–	2nd line
(3 + 3 + 2 = 8)	– –	1st, or beginning, line

8 *Examine the hexagram for changing lines:* If the constructed hexagram has changing lines, construct a second hexagram to the right of the first, or original, hexagram. Remember, changing lines turn into their opposites. All other lines remain the same.

Six is a broken line that changes into a solid line, number 7 (young yang). Nine is a solid line that changes into a broken line, number 8 (young yin).

Using the example from number 7, a second hexagram is constructed as follows:

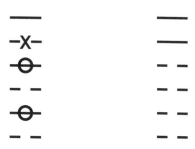

Original hexagram *(changing to)* 2nd hexagram

Note that there are never changing lines in the second hexagram.

9 *Find the number of your original hexagram in the* I Ching *Table:*

This table (page 13) is also the foldout in the back of Wilhelm's edition of the *I Ching*. First, find the lower trigram (bottom 3 lines) of the original hexagram in the left-hand column. Second, find the upper trigram (top 3 lines) in the top row. The number of the hexagram will be found where the row and column for the two trigrams intersect. If a second hexagram has been constructed, repeat the procedure.

Table 1. *Key for Identifying the Hexagrams*

TRIGRAMS UPPER ▶ LOWER ▼	Ch'ien ☰	Chên ☳	K'an ☵	Kên ☶	K'un ☷	Sun ☴	Li ☲	Tui ☱
Ch'ien ☰	1	34	5	26	11	9	14	43
Chên ☳	25	51	3	27	24	42	21	17
K'an ☵	6	40	29	4	7	59	64	47
Kên ☶	33	62	39	52	15	53	56	31
K'un ☷	12	16	8	23	2	20	35	45
Sun ☴	44	32	48	18	46	57	50	28
Li ☲	13	55	63	22	36	37	30	49
Tui ☱	10	54	60	41	19	61	38	58

The example given in item 8 on page 12 yields the following result:

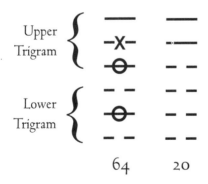

In the original hexagram (see page 12), the lower trigram is K'an and the upper trigram is

Li. Following K'an across and Li down, the
number 64 (Wei Chi/Before Completion) is
revealed.

The second hexagram (see page 12) is composed of K'un and Sun. Their intersection
reveals number 20 (Kuan/Contemplation).

10 *Read the* I Ching *text for the original hexagram:* Begin by

reading the number and name of the hexagram,
and stop at the heading for The Lines. There
are no unimportant parts, so do not skip anything. Do not worry if words and images are
difficult to understand. Read the text and
absorb what you can. Each time you consult
the *I Ching*, a greater amount of information
will be imparted to you. Through repetition,
the material becomes familiar and more mean-
ingful.

11 *If changing lines are present, read the appropriate lines:* Our

example, Hexagram 64 (Wei Chi/Before
Completion), contains changing lines in the
2nd, 4th, and 5th places. Under the heading,
The Lines, read 9 in the 2nd place, 9 in the
4th place, and 6 in the 5th place. Read only
the changing lines. Remember, the bottom
(1st) line is the beginning line.

A square (☐) or a circle (○) preceding a
changing line in the text indicates a ruling line.
A square (☐) indicates a constituting, or
Earthly, ruler. A circle (○) indicates a governing, or heavenly, ruler. These ruling lines, par-
ticularly the heavenly ruler, should be considered more significant and given greater consid-
eration than lines without symbols (*I Ching*,
pp. 364-365).

12 *Read the* I Ching *text for the
second hexagram:* Begin by reading the number and name of the hexagram,
and stop at the heading for The Lines. Note,
once again, that there are never changing lines
in the second hexagram.

13 *If changing lines are not present in the original hexagram,
read the material only up to The Lines:*
You will not construct a second hexagram.

HOW TO CONSULT
THE NUCLEAR HEXAGRAM

The nuclear hexagram can be consulted when more information is needed to answer your question.

The bottom two lines of a hexagram represent Earth; the middle two lines represent Humankind; the top two lines represent Heaven.

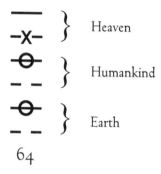

64

Each hexagram contains two nuclear trigrams, upper and lower.

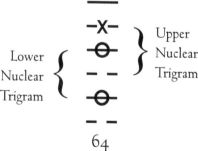

64

A nuclear hexagram is constructed from the original hexagram by combining two lines of Humankind with one line of Earth (lower

nuclear trigram), and two lines of Humankind
with one line of Heaven (upper nuclear trigram).

$$\begin{array}{c}
\text{— —} \\
\text{———} \\
\text{— —} \\
\text{———} \\
\text{— —} \\
\text{———}
\end{array}$$

63   (Chi Chi/After
Completion)

This construction allows us to magnify humankind's perspective within the situation, in order
to see the origin of the question. Read as much
of the hexagram as you need to gain clarity.

ANOTHER WAY THE *I CHING* MAY BE USEFUL

The six lines of the hexagram represent six
(of seven) chakras (energy centers) of the
human body. There are seven chakras and only
six lines. When the first six chakras are in
order, or balanced, the seventh (crown) chakra
is attained. When you are in the seventh
chakra, you are at peace. You have obtained
your objective and there is no other information needed. Therefore, the *I Ching* concerns
itself only with the first six chakras. The following list identifies the six chakras with lines
of a hexagram:

Mind	6th, or top, line
Communication	5th line
Love	4th line
Power	3rd line
Sex, Reproduction	2nd line
Security	1st, or beginning, line

Security concerns your ability to feed, clothe, and shelter yourself.

Sex, Reproduction concerns those things that attract the type of people you will meet and with whom you will reproduce. It includes your mores, your values, as well as the clothes you wear, the car you drive, the music you like, etc.

Power concerns your self-image. You have an image of what it is that you think people see when they look at you. If you are unhappy with that image, a power problem ensues.

Love concerns your ability to assist nature.

Communication concerns your ability to describe your emotional criteria to another person.

Mind concerns your ability to put the world in order; to be at peace with yourself.

Make a list of the six chakras, as follows:

	A	B	C
Mind		▬▬▬	▬▬▬
Communication		▬▬▬	▬▬▬
Love		▬ ▬	▬▬▬
Power		▬ ▬	▬ ▬
Sex, Reproduction		▬ ▬	▬ ▬
Security		▬▬▬	▬▬▬

Beginning with security, describe each of your chakras as either creative (——) or receptive (– –). Draw either a solid or a broken line next to each chakra, constructing a hexagram (as in column B). Do not take a great deal of time considering each chakra. Your initial impulse is generally accurate. This process will reveal your present emotional situation.

Read the names of the 64 hexagrams under "Contents" in the *I Ching*. Choose the title that best describes the emotional situation in which you would prefer to be. Construct your selected hexagram to the right of your first hexagram (as in column C).

In this example, in order for the second hexagram to follow the first, the 4th line would have to be a changing line (love chakra). Changing lines are important. They are the changes that need to be understood in order to successfully change into the preferred hexa-gram, or emotional situation.

Find the numbers of the hexagrams by using Table 1. Read the appropriate hexagrams and changing line(s).

A WORD ABOUT THE YARROW-STALK ORACLE

The *I Ching* is founded on the plant oracle. Plants contain the source of life. Our common yarrow (*Achillea millefolium*) was a sacred plant in China and its nature was round and spiritual. The stalks were taken from the yarrow plant and used in the consulting process through manipulation, or division.

Yarrow stalks are still employed to consult the *I Ching* today. The process is much lengthier than with coins, but the longer ritual provides the inquirer with more time to meditate upon and consider the question. Complete instructions for the yarrow-stalk oracle are provided in the back of the *I Ching* (pp. 721-723), along with instructions for the coin oracle (pp. 723-724).

3

Concordance

COLORS

"…correct (yellow)…"
—FOREWORD, p. xxxi

"…valuable (golden)."
—FOREWORD, p. xxxi

"Yellow is the color of the earth and of the middle; it is the symbol of that which is reliable and genuine."
—BOOK I, p. 15

"Midnight blue is the color of heaven; yellow is the color of the earth."
—BOOK I, p. 15

"Yellow is the color of the middle. It indicates that which is correct and in line with duty."
—BOOK I, p. 131

"The Creative… is deep red…"
—BOOK II, p. 275

"Deep red is the intensified color of the light principle (in the text itself, midnight blue is the color of the Creative, according with the color of the sky)."
—BOOK II, p. 275

"Among the various kinds of soil [the
Receptive] is the black."
—BOOK II, p. 276

"Black is intensified darkness."
—BOOK II, p. 276

"In the text of the *I Ching*, the color of the
Receptive is yellow…"
—BOOK II, p. 276, footnote

"…Chêng K'ang Ch'êng says: 'Heaven is blue-
black, the earth is yellow…'"
—BOOK II, p. 332

"Yellow is the color of the middle and of
moderation."
—BOOK III, p. 395

"Heaven is black and earth yellow."
—BOOK III, p. 395

"Black, or rather dark blue, is the color of
heaven, and yellow that of the earth. (It should
be noted that the color symbolism here differs
from that in the comments on the eight
trigrams, where the Creative is said to be red
and the Receptive black, i.e., dark.)"
—BOOK III, p. 396

CROSS THE GREAT WATERS

"...making the necessary decision and of
surmounting the danger."
—BOOK I, p. 25

"...[begin] dangerous enterprises..."
—BOOK I, p. 29

"...difficult and dangerous tasks...can be
accomplished."
—BOOK I, p. 56

"...accomplish even difficult undertakings..."
—BOOK I, p. 65

"...not recoil from work and danger..."
—BOOK I, p. 76

"...undertake even great and difficult labors..."
—BOOK I, p. 111

"...undertakings are possible, and even
difficult and dangerous enterprises
will succeed."
—BOOK I, p. 162

"...co-operation in great general
undertakings..."
—BOOK I, p. 228

"...undertake even the most
dangerous things..."
—BOOK I, p. 236

"...take the decisive step..."
—BOOK I, p. 251

"...To rely on wood is productive of merit."
—BOOK II, p. 333

"Through progress the work is accomplished."
—BOOK III, p. 411

"...dangerous and decisive undertakings..."
—BOOK III, p. 601

"To rely on wood is productive of merit."
—BOOK III, p. 690

"The idea of crossing the great water derives
from Sun (wood) and K'an (water)."
—BOOK III, p. 691

"One makes use of the hollow of a
wooden boat."
—BOOK III, p. 699

DURATION

"…the power of persisting in time…"
—BOOK I, p. 3

"…moving with untiring power,…a
movement that never stops or slackens…"
—BOOK I, pp. 6-7

"By holding fast to what is right…"
—BOOK I, p. 15

"Duration is a state whose movement is not
worn down by hindrances. It is not a state of
rest, for mere standstill is regression. Duration
is rather the self-contained and therefore self-
renewing movement of an organized, firmly
integrated whole, taking place in accordance
with immutable laws and beginning
anew at every ending."
—BOOK I, p. 126

"In that which gives things their duration, we
can come to understand the nature of all
beings in heaven and on earth."
—BOOK I, p. 127

"Thunder and wind: the image of DURATION."
—BOOK I, p. 127

"Fruit is a symbol of duration in change."
—BOOK II, p. 275

"The secret of tao in this world of the mutable,
the world of light—the realm of yang—is to
keep the changes in motion in such a manner
that no stasis occurs and an unbroken
coherence is maintained. He who succeds in
endowing his work with this regenerative
power creates something organic, and the
thing so created is enduring."
—BOOK II, p. 300

"The secret of action lies in duration."
—BOOK II, p. 326

"Through continuity [the clans of the Yellow
Emperor, of Yao, and of Shun]
achieved duration."
—BOOK II, p. 332

"Duration means that which always is."
—BOOK III, p. 545

"Duration means long-lasting."
—BOOK III, p. 545

"DURATION means that which lasts long."
—BOOK III, p. 546

"DURATION brings about firmness of
character. DURATION shows manifold
experiences without satiety. DURATION brings
about unity of character."
—BOOK III, p. 546

"Gentle and in motion. The strong and the
weak all correspond: this signifies duration."
—BOOK III, p. 546

"The course of heaven and earth is enduring
and long and never ends."
—BOOK III, p. 546

"If we meditate on what gives duration to a
thing, we can understand the nature of heaven
and earth and of all beings."
—BOOK III, p. 546

THE FIELD OF ACTION

"...greatness is the field of action of the sage."
—BOOK II, p. 286

"...good fortune and misfortune..."
—BOOK II, p. 317

"Good fortune and misfortune create the great field of action."
—BOOK II, p. 319

"The 'great field of action' are the regulations and rules instituted by the sages in order to obtain good fortune for men and to avoid misfortune."
—BOOK II, p. 319

"That which raises [things] up and sets them forth before all people on earth is called the field of action."
—BOOK II, p. 323

THE FIRST ATTRIBUTE:
SUBLIMITY

"The Chinese word here rendered by 'sublime'
means literally 'head,' 'origin,' 'great.' "
—BOOK I, p. 4

"To sublimity, which, as the fundamental
principle, embraces all the other attributes, [is
linked] love."
—BOOK I, p. 5

"[Sublimity] shows the love that acquiesces
trustingly in every situation and, out of its
store of inner kindness, manifests itself in good
will toward all men, thereby attaining
sublimity, the root of all good."
—BOOK II, p. 296

"Great indeed is the sublimity of the Creative,
to which all beings owe their beginning and
which permeates all heaven."
—BOOK III, p. 370

"The...attribute [sublimity]..., which, as the
primal cause of all that exists, forms the most
important and most inclusive attribute of the
Creative. The root meaning of the Chinese
word for it—*yüan*—is literally 'head.' "
—BOOK III, p. 370

"Of all that is good, sublimity is supreme."
—Book III, p. 376

"…the four fundamental attributes of the
[Creative] are related to the four cardinal
virtues of Chinese ethics. Sublimity is
correlated with humaneness…"
—Book III, p. 376

The Second Attribute:
Success

"The beginning of all things lies still in the
beyond in the form of ideas that have yet to
become real. But the Creative…has power to
lend form to these archetypes of ideas. This is
indicated in the word success, and the process
is represented by an image from nature: 'The
clouds pass and the rain does its work, and all
individual beings flow into their forms.' "
—Book I, p. 4

"Here it is shown that the way to success lies in apprehending and giving actuality to the way of the universe [tao], which, as a law running through end and beginning, brings about all phenomena in time."
—BOOK I, p. 5

"To the attribute success are linked the mores, which regulate and organize the expressions of love and thereby make them successful."
—BOOK I, pp. 5-6

"Modesty creates success."
—BOOK I, p. 63

"Human life on Earth is conditioned and unfree, and when man recognizes this limitation and makes himself dependent upon the harmonious and beneficent forces of the cosmos, he achieves success."
—BOOK I, p. 119

"Times of adversity are the reverse of times of success..."
—BOOK I, p. 181

"[Success] pictures wisdom and love, excluding no person or thing; these are regulated by the mores, which do not allow one to be carried away into anything improper or one-sided, and therefore have success."
—BOOK II, p. 296

" 'The clouds pass and the rain does its work,
and all individual beings flow into their forms.'
This explains the expression 'success.' The
success of the creative activity is revealed in the
gift of water, which causes the germination and
sprouting of all living things."
—BOOK III, pp. 370-371

"Succeeding is the coming together of all that
is beautiful."
—BOOK III, p. 376

"…the four fundamental attributes of
[the Creative] are related to the four cardinal
virtues of Chinese ethics. …success [is
correlated] with the mores…"
—BOOK III, p. 376

"…form."
—BOOK III, p. 496

THE THIRD ATTRIBUTE: FURTHERING

"The German word used here is *fördernd*, literally rendered by 'furthering.' It occurs again and again as a key word in Wilhelm's rendering of the Chinese text. To avoid extreme awkwardness, the phrase 'is favorable' is occasionally used as an alternative."
—BOOK I, p. 4, footnote 2

"...literally, 'creating that which accords with the nature of a given being'..."
—BOOK I, p. 5

"The attribute furthering is correlated with justice, which creates the conditions in which each receives that which accords with his being, that which is due him and which constitutes his happiness."
—BOOK I, p. 6

"The effect of wisdom, love, and justice is shown in [furthering]. On the basis of all-embracing wisdom, the regulations springing from a love of the world can be so shaped that all goes well for everyone and no mistakes are made. This is what furthers."
—BOOK II, p. 296

"Furtherance is the agreement of
all that is just."
—Book III, p. 376

"...the four fundamental attributes of the
[Creative] are related to the four cardinal
virtues of Chinese ethics. ...furtherance [is
correlated] with justice..."
—Book III, p. 376

THE FOURTH ATTRIBUTE:
PERSEVERANCE

"...(literally, 'correct and firm')."
—Book I, p. 5

"The attribute perseverance is correlated with
wisdom, which discerns the immutable laws of
all that happens and can therefore bring about
enduring conditions."
—Book I, p. 6

"…steadfastness and intensified, unswerving
devotion to duty."
—BOOK I, p. 177

"…steadfastness…"
—BOOK I, p. 218

"…decisiveness…"
—BOOK I, p. 221

"Resolute discipline…"
—BOOK I, p. 221

"…a firm and correct attitude of mind…"
—BOOK I, p. 223

" [Perseverance] shows the harmony of mind,
perfect in wisdom, that rejoices in heaven and
understands its dispensations. This provides
the basis for perseverance."
—BOOK II, p. 296

"Good fortune and misfortune take effect
through perseverance. The tao of heaven and
earth becomes visible through perseverance.
The tao of sun and moon becomes bright
through perseverance. All movements
under heaven become uniform
through perseverance."
—BOOK II, p. 326

"…(lastingness and integrity)."
—BOOK III, p. 372

"Perseverance is the foundation of all actions."
—BOOK III, p. 376

"…the four fundamental attributes of
[the Creative] are related to the four cardinal
virtues of Chinese ethics. …perseverance [is
correlated] with wisdom."
—BOOK III, p. 376

"Perseverance means discipline."
—BOOK III, p. 421

THE FOUR DIRECTIONS:
NORTH, SOUTH, EAST, AND WEST
(see figure 2, pages 40–41)

"The time of toil and effort is indicated by the
west and the south, for west and south
symbolize the place where the Receptive works
for the Creative, as nature does in summer and
autumn....The east symbolizes the place
where a man receives orders from his master,
and the north the place where he
reports on what he has done."
—BOOK I, p. 12

"The southwest is the region of retreat, the
northeast that of advance."
—BOOK I, p. 151

"...to make our way back to ordinary
conditions as soon as possible; this is the
meaning of 'the southwest.'"
—BOOK I, p. 155

"...activity (this is the meaning of
'the south')..."
—BOOK I, p. 178

"...in several of the sixty-four hexagrams, the
southwest represents the period of work and
fellowship, while the northeast stands for the

time of solitude, when the old is brought to an end and the new is begun."
—Book II, p. 271

"K'un is in the southwest, it is the earth, that which is level; friends are there. Kên is in the northeast, it is the mountain, that which is steep; there it is lonely."
—Book III, pp. 579-580

"In the northeast (north means danger, northeast means mountain) one comes to an impassable road, leading no farther."
—Book III, p. 581

"Tui is in the west, which indicates evening; Ch'ien is in the northwest, which indicates night."
—Book III, p. 605

"Departure toward the south means work. The south is the region of the heavens between Sun and K'un…"
—Book III, p. 621

"The trigram K'an stands in the north, where gloom prevails."
—Book III, p. 626

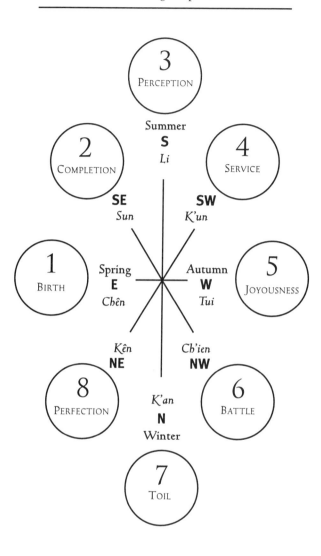

Figure 2. Sequence of Later Heaven, or Inner-World, arrangement. (Worldly progression in which the trigrams manifest themselves in the cycle of the year.)

1. BIRTH
    • Eternity of the end comes forth in accordance with fixed laws • Ascent • Beginning of life • Symbolizes the place where a man receives orders from his master

2. COMPLETION
    • The flow of beings into their forms; baptism and giving life

3. PERCEPTION
    • Activity • Indicates time of toil and effort • Work • Region of the heavens between Sun and K'un

4. SERVICE
    • The earth, that which is level; friends are there • Represents the period of work and fellowship • Region of retreat • Making our way back to ordinary conditions as soon as possible

5. JOYOUSNESS
    • Place of the white tiger • Metal • Evening • Indicates the time of toil and effort • The end of life • Decline • Eternity of the end reaches the end of its activity in accordance with fixed laws • Impartial justice • Place and time of death

6. BATTLE
    • Night

7. TOIL
    • Danger • Symbolizes the place where a man reports on what he has done • Where gloom prevails

8. PERFECTION
    • Mountain, that which is steep; there it is lonely • Region of advance • Stands for the time of solitude, when the old is brought to an end and the new is begun • Mysterious place where all things begin and end, where death and birth pass one into the other

"The trigram Tui…stands in the west, the
place of the white tiger."
—BOOK III, p. 640

"The place of Kên is in the northeast, between
K'an in the north and Chên in the east.
It is the mysterious place where all things
begin and end, where death and birth
pass one into the other."
—BOOK III, p. 652

"…according to the arrangement of the eight
trigrams by King Wên [Inner-World
Arrangement], the upper trigram Chên
belongs in the east and denotes spring, the
beginning of life; the lower trigram Tui belongs
in the west and denotes autumn, the end of
life, and the two nuclear trigrams K'an and Li
represent the north (winter) and the
south (summer) respectively."
—BOOK III, p. 664

"THE MARRYING MAIDEN means the
beginning and end of humanity, as Chên in the
east means spring, ascent, and Tui in the
west means autumn, decline."
—BOOK III, p. 665

"The eternity of the end is suggested by the
trigram Chên, which comes forth in the east
(spring) and reaches the end of its activity in

the west (autumn), in accordance with fixed
laws. At that moment the death-dealing power
of autumn, which destroys all transient
beings, becomes active."
—BOOK III, p. 666

"Among the eight trigrams, Sun occupies the
southeast, between spring and summer. It
means the flowing of beings into their forms, it
means baptism and giving life."
—BOOK III, p. 680

"…impartial justice…[is] symbolized by the
west (metal, autumn), with which the eighth
cyclic sign, Kêng (rendered as 'change'),
is associated."
—BOOK III, p. 683

"Killing and judging are attributes of Tui.*"
The footnote in Wilhelm's book reads as
follows: "*As the symbol of the west and of
autumn, the place and time of death."
—BOOK III, p. 700

THE GREAT MAN

"Because he sees with great clarity causes and effects, he completes the six steps at the right time and mounts toward heaven on them at the right time, as though on six dragons."
—BOOK I, p. 4

"In relation to the human sphere, …the great man brings peace and security to the world through his activity in creating order: 'He towers high above the multitude of beings, and all lands are united in peace.' "
—BOOK I, p. 5

"…what distinguishes [the great man] from the others is his seriousness of purpose, his unqualified reliability, and the influence he exerts on his environment without conscious effort. Such a man is destined to gain great influence and to set the world in order."
—BOOK I, p. 8

"A twofold possibility is presented to the great man: he can soar to the heights and play an important part in the world, or he can withdraw into solitude and develop himself. He can go the way of the hero or that of the holy sage who seeks seclusion."
—BOOK I, p. 9

"...an impartial man whose authority is great enough to terminate the conflict amicably or assure a just decision."
—BOOK I, p. 29

"The great man fosters and takes care of superior men, in order to take care of all men through them."
—BOOK I, p. 108

"The great man continues the work of nature in the human world. Through the clarity of his nature he causes the light to spread farther and farther and to penetrate the nature of man ever more deeply."
—BOOK I, pp. 119-120

"...a man equal to the situation..."
—BOOK I, p. 151

"...authoritative people."
—BOOK I, p. 178

"...[the] inner wealth [of the really great man] is inexhaustible; the more that people draw from him, the greater his wealth becomes."
—BOOK I, p. 188

"The great man changes like a tiger.
Even before he questions the oracle
He is believed."
—Book I, p. 192

"…an eminent man who is capable
of creating order."
—Book I, p. 221

"This means a man who has the character of a
dragon and is moderate and correct. Even in
ordinary speech he is reliable. Even in ordinary
actions he is careful. He does away with what
is false and preserves his integrity. He improves
his era and does not boast about it. His
character is influential and transforms men."
—Book III, p. 380

"…a man who has the qualities of a ruler."
—Book III, p. 380

"The great man accords in his character with
heaven and earth; in his light, with the sun and
moon; in his consistency, with the four
seasons; in the good and evil fortune that
he creates, with gods and spirits. When he
acts in advance of heaven, heaven does not
contradict him. When he follows heaven,
he adapts himself to the time of heaven. If

heaven itself does not resist him, how
much less do men, gods, and spirits!"
—BOOK III, pp. 382-383

"The reference to 'the great man' in the
Judgment always relates to the fifth place."
—BOOK III, p. 579

"...a man of rank."
—BOOK III, p. 583

"The strong line in the fifth place represents
the king, the great man..."
—BOOK III, p. 615

THE HOLY MAN

"The holy man, who understands the
mysteries of creation inherent in end and
beginning, in death and life, in dissolution and
growth, and who understands how these polar
opposites condition one another, becomes
superior to the limitations of the transitory.
For him, the meaning of time is that in it the
stages of growth can unfold in a clear
sequence. He is mindful at every moment and
uses the six stages of growth as if they were six
dragons (the image attributed to the individual
lines) on which he mounts toward heaven.
This is the sublimity and success of the
Creative as it shows itself in man."
—BOOK III, p. 371

" 'He towers high above the multitude of
beings, and all lands are united in peace.' This
describes the creative power of the holy man,
who makes it possible for everything to attain
its appropriate place, thus bringing about
peace on earth, when he occupies
an eminent ruling place."
—BOOK III, p. 372

"Those below look toward [the holy man] and
are transformed. He affords them a view of the
divine way of heaven, and the four seasons do
not deviate from their rule. Thus the holy man

uses the divine way to give instruction, and the whole world submits to him."
—Book III, p. 486

"The holy man knows the laws of heaven. He reveals them to the people, and his predictions come true. Just as the seasons of the year move under divine and immutable laws, so events do not deviate from the course he prophesies. Thus he uses his knowledge of the divine ways to teach the people, and the people trust him and look up to him."
—Book III, p. 487

"The holy man provides nourishment for men of worth and thus reaches the whole people."
—Book III, p. 521

"The holy man stimulates the hearts of men, and the world attains peace and rest."
—Book III, p. 541

"The holy man remains forever in his course, and the world reshapes itself to completion."
—Book III, p. 546

"The holy man cooks in order to sacrifice to God the Lord, and he cooks feasts in order to nourish the holy and the worthy."
—Book III, p. 642

THE INFERIOR MAN

"The conduct of the 'inferior man'—the
lower-class individual—was governed by law."
—BOOK I, p. 6, footnote 5

"The inferior man is not ashamed of
unkindness and does not shrink from injustice.
If no advantage beckons he makes no effort. If
he is not intimidated he does not improve
himself, but if he is made to behave correctly
in small matters he is careful in large ones."
—BOOK I, pp. 89-90, footnote 2

"...the inferior man thinks to himself,
'Goodness in small things has no value,' and
so neglects it. He thinks, 'Small sins do no
harm,' and so does not give them up. Thus his
sins accumulate until they can no longer be
covered up, and his guilt becomes so great that
it can no longer be wiped out."
—BOOK I, p. 90, footnote 2

"The inferior man himself fares best when
held under control by a superior man."
—BOOK I, p. 96

"He who cultivates the inferior parts of his
nature is an inferior man."
—BOOK I, p. 108

"…'In what is small' — here equivalent to 'in
the inferior man'…"
—BOOK I, p. 131

"The inferior man works through power.
The superior man does not act thus."
"Whereas an inferior man revels in power
when he comes into possession of it, the
superior man never makes this mistake."
—BOOK I, pp. 134-135

"Difficulties and obstructions throw a man
back upon himself. …the inferior man seeks to
put the blame on other persons,
bewailing his fate…"
—BOOK I, p. 152

"The dark trigrams have two rulers and one
subject. This is the way of the inferior man."
—BOOK II, p. 337

"…whatever is inferior is in every case
something external or objective."
—BOOK III, p. 397

"Boylike contemplation.
For an inferior man, no blame.
For a superior man, humiliation."
—BOOK III, p. 487

"The boylike contemplation of the six at the
beginning is the way of inferior people."
—Book III, p. 487

THE SUPERIOR MAN

"…'superior man,' *chün-tzu* [is] a term which
meant an aristocrat in early Chou China."
—Preface, p. xv

"The doctrine of the Mean shows that the
'way of the superior man' leads to harmony
between heaven, man, and earth."
—Introduction, p. lix, footnote 22

"Obedience to the code of *li* [moral conduct]
was entirely self-imposed as regards the
'superior man,' who in feudal times
was always a man of rank."
—Book I, p. 6, footnote 5

"The movement of heaven is full of power.
Thus the superior man makes himself
strong and untiring."
—BOOK I, p. 6 and Book III, p. 373

"If the superior man undertakes
something and tries to lead,
He goes astray;
But if he follows, he finds guidance."
—BOOK I, p. 11 and Book III, p. 386

"The superior man lets himself be guided; he
does not go ahead blindly, but learns from the
situation what is demanded of him and then
follows this intimation from fate."
—BOOK I, p. 12

"The earth's condition is receptive devotion.
Thus the superior man who
has breadth of character
Carries the outer world."
—BOOK I, p. 12, and BOOK III, p. 389

"The earth in its devotion carries all things,
good and evil, without exception. In the same
way the superior man gives to his character
breadth, purity, and sustaining power, so that
he is able both to support and to bear
with people and things."
—BOOK I, p. 13

"...the superior man
Brings order out of confusion."
—Book I, p. 17 and Book III, p. 400

"...the superior man has to arrange and
organize the inchoate profusion of such times
of beginning, just as one sorts out silk threads
from a knotted tangle and binds
them into skeins."
—Book I, p. 17

"...the superior man, discerning the seeds of
coming events, prefers to renounce a wish
rather than to provoke failure and humiliation
by trying to force its fulfillment."
—Book I, p. 19

"...the superior man fosters his character
By thoroughness in all that he does."
—Book I, p. 21and Book III, p. 408

"The image of WAITING.
Thus the superior man eats and drinks,
Is joyous and of good cheer."
—Book I, p. 25 and Book III, p. 412

"...in all his transactions the superior man
Carefully considers the beginning."
—Book I, p. 29 and Book III, p. 417

"...the superior man increases his masses
By generosity toward the people."
—BOOK I, p. 33 and Book III, p. 422

"...the superior man...never
loses his dignity."
—BOOK I, p. 38

"...the superior man
Refines the outward aspect of his nature."
—BOOK I, p. 41 and Book III, p. 432

"...the superior man discriminates
between high and low,
And thereby fortifies the
thinking of the people."
—BOOK I, p. 45 and Book III, p. 437

"...the superior man falls back upon
his inner worth
In order to escape the difficulties."
—BOOK I, p. 53 and Book III, p. 448

"When, owing to the influence of inferior
men, mutual mistrust prevails in public
life...the superior man...does not allow
himself to be tempted by dazzling offers to take
part in public activities. ... He...hides his
worth and withdraws into seclusion."
—BOOK I, p. 53

"…the superior man does not forget danger in
his security, nor ruin when he is well
established, nor confusion when
his affairs are in order."
—Book I, p. 55

"…the superior man organizes the clans
And makes distinctions between things."
—Book I, p. 57 and Book III, p. 453

"…the superior man curbs evil
and furthers good,
And thereby obeys the benevolent
will of heaven."
—Book I, p. 60 and Book III, p. 458

"The superior man carries things through."
—Book I, p. 63 and Book III, p. 462

"When a man holds a high position and is
nevertheless modest, he shines with the light
of wisdom; if he is in a lowly position and is
modest, he cannot be passed by. Thus the
superior man can carry out his work to
the end without boasting of
what he has achieved."
—Book I, p. 64

"…the superior man reduces that
which is too much,
And augments that which is too little.

He weighs things and makes them equal."
—Book I, p. 64 and Book III, p. 463

"The superior man…equalizes the extremes
that are the source of social discontent and
thereby creates just and equable conditions."
—Book I, p. 64

"A superior man of modesty and merit
Carries things to conclusion."
—Book I, p. 65 and Book III, p. 464

"In his association with those above him, the
superior man does not flatter. In his
association with those beneath him,
he is not arrogant."
"The superior man knows what is hidden
and what is evident.
He knows weakness, he knows
strength as well.
Hence the myriads look up to him."
—Book I, p. 70

"…the superior man at nightfall
Goes indoors for rest and recuperation."
—Book I, p. 72 and Book III, p. 473

"…the superior man stirs up the people
And strengthens their spirit."
—Book I, p. 76 and Book III, p. 479

"...the superior man is inexhaustible
In his will to teach,
And without limits
In his tolerance and protection of the people."
—Book I, p. 79 and Book III, p. 482-483

"...a superior personality...will have a view of
the real sentiments of the great mass of
humanity and therefore cannot be
deceived;...he will impress the people so
profoundly, by his mere existence and by the
impact of his personality, that they will be
swayed by him as the grass by the wind."
—Book I, p. 83

"...a superior man...must not content himself
with a shallow, thoughtless view of prevailing
forces; he must contemplate them as a
connected whole and try to understand them."
—Book I, p. 84

"Liberated from his ego [the superior man]
contemplates the laws of life and so realizes
that knowing how to become free of blame is
the highest good."
—Book I, p. 85

"Fire at the foot of the mountain:
The image of GRACE.
Thus does the superior man proceed
When clearing up current affairs.

But he dare not decide controversial
issues in this way."
—BOOK I, p. 91 and Book III, p. 496

"…the superior man acquaints himself with
many sayings of antiquity
And many deeds of the past,
In order to strengthen his character thereby."
—BOOK I, p. 105 and Book III, p. 516

"The great man fosters and takes care of
superior men, in order to take care of all men
through them. Mencius says about this: If we
wish to know whether anyone is superior or
not, we need only observe what part of his
being he regards as especially important. The
body has superior and inferior, important and
unimportant parts. We must not injure
important parts for the sake of the
unimportant, nor must we injure the superior
parts for the sake of the inferior. He who
cultivates the inferior parts of his nature is an
inferior man. He who cultivates the superior
parts of his nature is a superior man."
—BOOK I, p. 108

"…the superior man is careful of his words
And temperate in eating and drinking."
—BOOK I, p. 108 and Book III, p. 521

"…the superior man, when he stands alone,
Is unconcerned,
And if he has to renounce the world,
He is undaunted."
—Book I, p. 112 and Book III, p. 527

"…the superior man walks in lasting virtue
And carries on the business of teaching."
—Book I, p. 116 and Book III, p. 532

"Water reaches its goal by flowing continually.
It fills up every depression before it flows on.
The superior man follows its example; he is
concerned that goodness should be an
established attribute of character rather than
an accidental and isolated occurrence. So
likewise in teaching others everything depends
on consistency, for it is only through repetition
that the pupil makes the material his own."
—Book I, p. 116

"To the superior man it makes no difference
whether death comes early or late. He
cultivates himself, awaits his allotted time, and
in this way secures his fate."
—Book I, pp. 120-121

"…the superior man encourages
people to approach him
By his readiness to receive them."
"(Literally, 'Thus the superior man receives

people by virtue of emptiness.')"
—BOOK I, p. 123 and Book III, p. 542

"...the superior man stands firm
And does not change his direction."
—BOOK I, p. 127 and Book III, p. 547

"...the independence of the superior man is
not based on rigidity and immobility of
character. He always keeps abreast of the time
and changes with it. What endures is the
unswerving directive, the inner law of his
being, which determines all his actions."
—BOOK I, p. 127

"...the superior man keeps the inferior man at
a distance,
Not angrily but with reserve."
—BOOK I, p. 130 and Book III, p. 551

"In retreating the superior man is intent on
taking his departure willingly and in all
friendliness. He easily adjusts his mind to
retreat, because in retreating he does not have
to do violence to his convictions."
—BOOK I, p. 132

"... the superior man does not tread
upon paths
That do not accord with established order."
—BOOK I, p. 134 and Book III, p. 557

"…in times of great power the superior man avoids doing anything that is not in harmony with the established order."
—BOOK I, p. 134

"The inferior man works through power. The superior man does not act thus."
"Whereas an inferior man revels in power when he comes into possession of it, the superior man never makes this mistake. He is conscious at all times of the danger of pushing ahead regardless of circumstances, and therefore renounces in good time the empty display of force."
—BOOK I, pp. 134-135

"…the superior man himself Brightens his bright virtue."
—BOOK I, p. 137 and Book III, p. 561

"The image of DARKENING OF THE LIGHT. Thus does the superior man live with the great mass:
He veils his light, yet still shines."
—BOOK I, p. 140 and Book III, p. 566

"…the superior man has substance in his words And duration in his way of life."
—BOOK I, p. 144 and Book III, p. 571

"...amid all fellowship
The superior man retains his individuality."
—BOOK I, p. 148 and Book III, p. 575

"...the superior man turns his attention
to himself
And molds his character."
—BOOK I, p. 152 and Book III, p. 581

"Difficulties and obstructions throw a man
back upon himself. While the inferior man
seeks to put the blame on other persons,
bewailing his fate, the superior man seeks the
error within himself, and through this
introspection the external obstacle becomes
for him an occasion for inner
enrichment and education."
—BOOK I, p. 152

"...the superior man pardons mistakes
And forgives misdeeds."
—BOOK I, p. 155 and Book III, p. 586

"A thunderstorm has the effect of clearing the
air; the superior man produces a similar effect
when dealing with mistakes and sins of men
that induce a condition of tension. Through
clarity he brings deliverance. However, when
failings come to light, he does not dwell on
them; he simply passes over mistakes, the
unintentional transgressions, just as thunder

dies away. He forgives misdeeds, the
intentional transgressions, just as water
washes everything clean."
—BOOK I, p. 155

"...the superior man:
If he sees good, he imitates it;
If he has faults, he rids himself of them."
—BOOK I, p. 163 and Book III, p. 598

"The superior man sets his person at rest
before he moves; he composes his mind before
he speaks; he makes his relations firm before
he asks for something. By attending to these
matters, the superior man gains
complete security."
—BOOK I, p. 165

"...the superior man
Dispenses riches downward
And refrains from resting on his virtue."
—BOOK I, p. 167 and Book III, p. 604

"...the superior man begins to distribute while
he is accumulating. In the same way, in
developing his character he takes care not to
become hardened in obstinacy but to remain
receptive to impressions by help of strict and
continuous self-examination."
—BOOK I, p. 167

"The superior man is on his guard against what is not yet in sight and on the alert for what is not yet within hearing; therefore he dwells in the midst of difficulties as though they did not exist."
—Book I, p. 168

"The superior man is firmly resolved."
—Book I, p. 168 and Book III, p. 605

"...the superior man renews his weapons
In order to meet the unforseen."
—Book I, p. 175 and Book III, p. 616

"...the superior man of devoted character
Heaps up small things
In order to achieve something high and great."
—Book I, p. 179 and Book III, p. 621

"...the superior man is devoted in character
and never pauses in his progress."
—Book I, p. 179

"...the superior man stakes his life
On following his will."
—Book I, p. 182 and Book III, p. 625

"...the superior man encourages the
people at their work
And exhorts them to help one another."
—Book I, p. 186 and Book III, p. 631

"…the superior man
Sets the calendar in order
And makes the seasons clear."
—BOOK I, p. 190 and Book III, p. 637

"…the superior man consolidates his fate
By making his position correct."
—BOOK I, p. 194 and Book III, p. 643

"…in fear and trembling
The superior man sets his life in order
And examines himself."
—BOOK I, p. 198 and Book III, pp. 648-649

"The superior man is always filled with
reverence at the manifestation of God; he sets
his life in order and searches his heart, lest it
harbor any secret opposition to
the will of God."
—BOOK I, p. 198

"…the superior man
Does not permit his thoughts
To go beyond his situation."
—BOOK I, pp. 201-202 and Book III, p. 654

"…the superior man abides in
dignity and virtue,
In order to improve the mores."
—BOOK I, p. 205 and Book III, p. 659

"...the superior man
Understands the transitory
In the light of the eternity of the end."
—BOOK I, p. 209 and Book III, p. 665

"...the superior man decides lawsuits
And carries out punishments."
—BOOK I, p. 214 and Book III, p. 671

"...the superior man
Is clear-minded and cautious
In imposing penalties,
And protracts no lawsuits."
—BOOK I, p. 217 and Book III, p. 676

"...the superior man
Spreads his commands abroad
And carries out his undertakings."
—BOOK I, p. 221 and Book III, p. 681

"...the superior man joins with his friends
For discussion and practice."
—BOOK I, p. 224 and Book III, p. 686

"...a superior man can find no real satisfaction
in low pleasures."
—BOOK I, p. 225

"The Chinese word for limitation really denotes the joints that divide a bamboo stalk. In relation to ordinary life it means the thrift that sets fixed limits upon expenditures. In relation to the moral sphere it means the fixed limits that the superior man sets upon his actions—the limits of loyalty and disinterestedness."
—Book I, p. 231

"...the superior man
Creates number and measure,
And examines the nature of virtue and correct conduct."
—Book I, p. 232 and Book III, p. 696

"...the superior man discusses criminal cases
In order to delay executions."
—Book I, p. 236 and Book III, p. 700

"...superior man, when obliged to judge the mistakes of men, tries to penetrate their minds with understanding, in order to gain a sympathetic appreciation of the circumstances."
—Book I, p. 236

"Words and deeds are the hinge and bowspring of the superior man. As hinge and bowspring move, they bring honor or disgrace.

Through words and deeds the superior man
moves heaven and earth."
—Book I, p. 238

"…in his conduct the superior man gives
preponderance to reverence.
In bereavement he gives preponderance
to grief.
In his expenditures he gives preponderance
to thrift."
—Book I, p. 241 and Book III, p. 706

"…the superior man…must always fix his
eyes more closely and more directly on duty
than does the ordinary man, even though this
might make his behavior seem petty to the
outside world. He is exceptionally
conscientious in his actions. In bereavement
emotion means more to him than
ceremoniousness. In all his personal
expenditures he is extremely simple and
unpretentious. In comparison with the man of
the masses, all this makes him stand out as
exceptional. But the essential significance of his
attitude lies in the fact that in external matters
he is on the side of the lowly."
—Book I, p. 241

"...the superior man
Takes thought of misfortune
And arms himself against it in advance."
—BOOK I, p. 245 and Book III, p. 711

"...the superior man is careful
In the differentiation of things,
So that each finds its place."
—BOOK I, p. 249 and Book III, p. 716

"The light of the superior man is true."
—BOOK I, p. 251 and Book III, p. 717

"...it is the order of the Changes that the
superior man devotes himself to and that he
attains tranquillity by. It is the judgments on
the individual lines that the superior man takes
pleasure in and that he ponders on."
—BOOK II, p. 289

"...the superior man contemplates [the]
images in times of rest and meditates on the
judgments. When he undertakes something,
he contemplates the changes and
ponders on the oracles."
—BOOK II, p. 290

"...the way of the superior man, who sees not
only things but the tao of things, is rare."
—BOOK II, p. 299

"…the superior man, whenever he has to make or do something, consults the Changes, and he does so in words. It takes up his communications like an echo; neither far nor near, neither dark nor deep exist for it, and thus he learns of the things of the future."
—BOOK II, p. 314

"The light trigrams have one ruler and two subjects. They show the way of the superior man."
—BOOK II, p. 337

"THE CREATIVE…indicates the way of the superior man, and the fifth place, as that of the ruler, is his appropriate place."
—BOOK III, p. 369

"Because the superior man embodies humaneness, he is able to govern man. Because he brings about the harmonious working together of all that is beautiful, he is able to unite them through the mores. Because he furthers all beings, he is able to bring them into harmony through justice. Because he is persevering and firm, he is able to carry out all actions."
—BOOK III, p. 376

"The superior man acts in accordance with
[the] four virtues." [Sublimity, success,
furtherance, perseverance]
—BOOK III, p. 377

"The superior man acts in accordance with the
character that has become
perfected within him."
—BOOK III, p. 379

"The superior man learns in order to gather
material; he questions in order to sift it. Thus
he becomes generous in nature and
kindly in his actions."
—BOOK III, p. 380

"The Master said: The superior man improves
his character and labors at his task. It is through
loyalty and faith that he fosters his character. By
working on his words, so that they rest firmly
on truth, he makes his work enduring. He
knows how this is to be achieved and achieves
it; in this way he is able to plant the right seed.
He knows how it is to be brought to completion
and so completes it; thereby he is able to make
it truly enduring. For this reason he is not
proud in his superior position nor disappointed
in an inferior one. Thus he is creatively active
and, as circumstances demand, careful, so
that even in a dangerous situation
he does not make a mistake."
—BOOK III, pp. 380-381

"The superior man fosters his character and labors at his task, in order to do everything at the right time. Therefore he makes no mistake."
—BOOK III, p. 381

"Straightness means righting things; squareness means fulfillment of duty. The superior man is serious, in order to make his inner life straight; he does his duty, in order to make his outer life square."
—BOOK III, p. 393

"The superior man is yellow and moderate; thus he makes his influence felt in the outer world through reason.
He seeks the right place for himself and dwells in the essential.
His beauty is within, but it gives freedom to his limbs and expresses itself in his works.
This is the perfection of beauty."
—BOOK III, p. 395

"The right place sought by the superior man is found in the good form that makes him yield precedence to others and stay modestly in the background."
—BOOK III, p. 395

"…the *Book of Changes* is written only for
superior men."
—BOOK III, p. 397

"In his nature he is thoroughgoing, and clear
as a mountain spring. Hence [the superior
man] achieves a calmness in the face of danger
that emulates the great calmness of a mountain
on the edge of an abyss."
—BOOK III, p. 408

"… the superior man creates in society the
differences in rank that correspond with
differences in natural endowment, and in this
way fortifies the thinking of the people, who
are reassured when these differences
accord with nature."
—BOOK III, p. 437

"Order and clarity, in combination with
strength; central, correct, and in the
relationship of correspondence: this is the
correctness of the superior man. Only the
superior man is able to unite the wills of all
under heaven."
—BOOK III, p. 452

"The superior man, even when placed where
he serves, fills this position correctly and
unselfishly and finds the support he needs in

his ruler, the representative
of the heavenly principle."
—Book III, p. 452

"Modesty that is honored spreads radiance.
Modesty that is lowly cannot be ignored. This
is the end attained by the superior man."
—Book III, p. 462

" 'A superior man modest about his modesty'
is lowly in order to guard himself well."
—Book III, p. 463

" 'A superior man of modesty and merit': all
the people obey him."
—Book III, p. 464

"The superior man takes heed of the
alternation of increase and decrease, fullness
and emptiness; for it is the course of heaven."
—Book III, p. 501

"Water is constant in its flow; thus the
superior man is constant in his virtue, like the
firm line in the middle of the abyss. And just
as water flows on and on, so he makes use of
practice and repetition in the
business of teaching."
—Book III, p. 532

"The superior man keeps the inferior at a
distance by being as reserved and inaccessible
as heaven; thus he brings the
inferior man to a standstill."
—BOOK III, p. 552

"...the *Book of Changes* gives counsel not for
inferior men but only for the superior."
—BOOK III, p. 552

"It is the obligation of the superior man to
refrain from eating during his wanderings."
—BOOK III, p. 566

"The superior man always stays where he
belongs. He comes only into his own domain."
—BOOK III, p. 609

"The superior man alone is capable of being
oppressed without losing
the power to succeed."
—BOOK III, p. 625

GLOSSARY

chakra: Sanskrit term meaning wheel or disk; centers of energy, related to glandular and nervous systems

constituting (earthly) ruler: line that gives the hexagram its characteristic meaning

creative: light-giving, active, strong, and of the spirit

governing (heavenly) ruler: line that is always of good character

hexagram: sign consisting of six lines, either positive (——) or negative (— —)

Later Heaven, or Inner-World Arrangement: King Wen's arrangement of the eight trigrams. The trigrams are taken out of their grouing in pairs of opposites and shown in the temporal progression in which they manifest themselves in the phenomenal world in the cycle of the year. The cardinal points and the seasons are correlated.

nuclear trigrams: form the four middle lines of each hexagram. They overlap each other so that the middle line of the one falls within the other.

receptive: dark, yielding, devoted, represents earth

Tao: eternal law at work in all change, the course of things, the principle of the one in the many

trigram: sign consisting of three lines, either positive (——) or negative (– –)

yang: light, firm, spirit

yin: dark, yielding, matter

JILL RICHARDS began her spiritual studies in the 1960s, and accompanied her *I Ching* teacher, Walter Boye, from 1978–1979 on an incredible journey the length and breadth of America. It was during this journey that the country roads and highways became her classroom and an intensive study of the *I Ching* was her curriculum. Since then, she has assisted her teacher in conducting workshops and readings for seekers and students of the Book of Changes. She lives in Santa Barbara, California.